I0117942

Van Evrie John H.

Free Negroism

Or Results of Emancipation in the North and the West India Islands

Van Evrie John H.

Free Negroism
Or Results of Emancipation in the North and the West India Islands

ISBN/EAN: 9783337275013

Printed in Europe, USA, Canada, Australia, Japan

Cover: Foto ©Suzi / pixelio.de

More available books at **www.hansebooks.com**

No. 2. ANTI-ABOLITION TRACTS. Price 6 Cents.

FREE NEGROISM:

OR,

RESULTS OF EMANCIPATION

IN THE

NORTH AND THE WEST INDIA ISLANDS:

WITH

STATISTICS OF THE DECAY OF COMMERCE, IDLENESS
OF THE NEGRO, HIS RETURN TO SAVAGEISM.
AND THE EFFECT OF EMANCIPATION UPON
THE FARMING, MECHANICAL AND
LABORING CLASSES.

NEW YORK:

VAN EVRIE, HORTON & CO.,
No. 162 NASSAU STREET.

1862.

SECOND EDITION NOW READY.

☞ **All who would understand the Philosophy of the Negro Question, and see the horrors and evils of Abolition, should read this work.**

NEGROES AND NEGRO "SLAVERY:"

The First an Inferior Race—the Latter its Normal Condition.

By J. H. VAN EVRIE, M.D.

1 Vol., 12mo., pp. 339.   Price One Dollar.

ILLUSTRATED WITH FOUR CUTS, SHOWING THE DIFFERENCE BETWEEN WHITE MEN AND THE NEGRO.

The second edition of this work, so steady has been its sale, is already called for. The author has thoroughly revised it, and re-written an entire chapter. He assumes, as a starting point, that the subordinate position of the Negro, as always existing in American society, is not a condition of slavery at all, but the natural relation of an inferior to a superior race, and that whatever evils, if any, exist in Southern society, are referable to a failure to strictly embody the natural inferiority of the negro in the civil law, and not to any error in the fundamental organism or theory of that society, which is based on a great and everlasting truth. His work is divided into two parts. First, the specific and radical differences of the races are examined. The color, figure, hair, features, language, senses, brain, &c., of the Negro are shown to be only the more palpable specialities, out of a thousand similar ones, separating the Negro from the White Man. Why, when, or how the Creator saw fit to thus order things, the author regards as immaterial. He simply starts with the facts as they exist. After the Negro is shown to be a different human being, physically and mentally, his proper relations to the White Man are discussed; also, Mulattoism and its ultimate extinction, showing the impossibility of interunion, like cognate branches of the white race, a very important, and but little understood branch of the subject. The position assumed in this work is entirely new and distinct from that presented by any other writer; and founded, as it is, upon facts and unavoidable inferences from them, it is believed presents at last the true philosophy of this distracting question.

This work will be sent *by mail*, postage paid, for *One Dollar*.

Address,

VAN EVRIE, HORTON & CO.,
No 162 Nassau Street, New York.

FREE NEGROISM.

INTRODUCTORY.

GIGANTIO efforts are now being made to convince the people of the North that the overthrow of the present relations of the black and white races in the South, or what is mistakingly called "the Abolition of Slavery," would be a great benefit to all concerned—a benefit to the white race, to the negro race, and a grand step in the progress of civilization and Christianity. Now the simple TRUTH is the exact opposite of this. To overthrow the present relation of the races is to injure both the white man and the negro, and to inflict a deadly blow upon the cause of humanity, civilization, and Christianity. We only need to approach this subject in a spirit of candid inquiry, and to bring it to the touchstone of FACT. It is proposed to show in the following pages—

First—The effects of emancipation in the Northern States in the increase of crime, pauperism, and vice among the freed negroes;

Second—Its results in the West India Islands, where it has ruined production, destroyed commerce, and where the negro is fast relapsing into his original African savagism;

Third—The effect of Free Negroism upon the commerce, wealth, and business of the world, and especially upon *the white laboring and producing classes*, in producing a scarcity of tropical productions, and a consequent increase of price, thus allowing Negro Idleness to tax WHITE LABOR.

The inherent right or wrong of any measure may be fairly determined by its effect. That which produces crime, pauperism, immorality, poverty, and misery cannot in the nature of things be right. Theories vanish before the stern arbiter of FACTS, and to that unerring tribunal we appeal.

PART I.

FREE NEGROISM IN THE NORTH.

Soon after tho close of the Revolutionary War, a few individuals, mostly Quakers, commenced efforts for the emancipation of negroes then held as so-called slaves in all the States, except Massachusetts and Pennsylvania. It was a purely philanthropic movement, and had no more connection with politics than have the various missionary societies now in existence for diffusing Christianity in Burmah or China. Several States were induced to follow the example of Massachusetts and Pennsylvania, viz. :—Connecticut, Rhode Island, New Hampshire, Vermont, New York, and New Jersey. In New Jersey and New York emancipation was gradual, and though provided for in the former State in 1784, and in the latter in 1799, "slavery" did not entirely disappear until 1820-27. Here emancipation ceased, and did it ever occur to any one to inquire why, all of a sudden, this should be so? If it were a benefit to take from the negro the care and guidance of white men, why did not all the rest of the States follow the example? This question is better answered by the detail of a few facts. It was not without grave apprehensions as to the result that emancipation had been inaugurated, and it was only nine years after Pennsylvania had set the example in 1780, that Berjamin Franklin issued an Appeal for aid to his society "to form a plan for the promotion of industry, intelligence and morality among the free blacks." How far Franklin's benevolent scheme had fallen short of his anticipations, may be judged of from the fact that forty-seven years after Pennsylvania had passed her act of emancipation, *one third* of the convicts in her penitentiaries were negroes or mulattoes! Some of the other States were even in a worse condition, *one-half* of the convicts in the penitentiary of New Jersey being freed negroes. But Massachusetts was almost as badly off, and as a person's own admission against himself is the best evidence, we quote from the report of the "Boston Prison Discipline Society."

This benevolent Association included among its members, Rev. Francis Wayland, Rev. Austin Edwards, Rev. Leonard Woods, Rev. William Jenks, Rev. B. B. Wisner, Rev. Edward Beecher, Lewis Tappan, Esq., John Tappan, Esq., Hon. John Bliss, and Hon. Samuel M. Hopkins. In the First Annual Report of the Society, dated June 2, 1826, they enter into an investigation "of the progress of crime, with the causes of it," from which we make the following extract :

"DEGRADED CHARACTER OF THE COLORED POPULATION.—The first cause, "existing in society, of the frequency and increase of crime is *the degrad-* "*ed character of the colored population.* The facts, which are gathered "from the Penitentiaries, to show how great a proportion of the convicts "are colored, even in those States where the colored population is small, "show most strikingly, the connection between ignorance and vice."

The Report proceeds to sustain its assertions by statistics, which prove, that, in Massachusetts, where the free colored people constituted *one seventy-fourth* part of the population, they supplied *one-sixth* part of the convicts in her Penitentiary ; that in New York, where the free colored people constituted *one thirty fifth* part of the population, they supplied more than *one fourth* part of the convicts ; that, in Connecticut and Pennsylvania, where the colored people constituted *one thirty-fourth* part of the population, they supplied more than *one third* part of the convicts ; and that, in New Jersey, where the colored people constituted *one-thirteenth* part of the population, they supplied more than *one-third* part of the convicts.

In the second annual report of the Society, dated June 1st, 1827, the subject is again alluded to, and tables are given, showing more fully the degraded character of the freed negro population. "The returns from the several prisons," says the report, "show that the white convicts are remaining nearly the same, or are diminishing, while the colored convicts *are increasing*. At the same time the white population is increasing in the northern States much faster than the colored population." The following table is taken from the report :

	Whole number of Convicts.	Colored Convicts.	Proportion.
In Massachusetts..	313	50	1 to 6
In New York......	381	101	1 to 4
In New Jersey....	67	33	1 to 2

Were not these facts and statistics powerful arguments for arresting emancipation ? The other States, seeing its evil effects, took the alarm. Some of them passed laws prohibiting the freed negroes from coming within them, and it began to be declared that it was much easier and less expensive to manage "slaves" than free blacks. So great was the reaction which the disastrous experiment of emancipation produced, that some of the States passed laws prohibiting emancipation, unless upon condition that the freed negroes be removed from the country. Thus the Colonization Society arose. It was argued that if the negro could not rise to any respectable condition here, it might be owing to the prejudice against his color and the social outlawry visited upon him. To place him, therefore, in a position where none of these influences could affect him, it was proposed to colonize all who were freed, and, for many years, negro "philanthropy" exhausted itself in this direction. The Society was popular at one time, even at the South. It was regarded by some as the agent or means which would gradually do away with "slavery," and by others as simply an organization to get rid of the incubus of freed negroes. In 1826 the Society, by a resolution, declared itself as "not designing to interfere with slavery where it existed, nor yet as endeavoring to perpetuate its existence." This did not suit the more radical members, and Wm. Lloyd Garrison, Jas. G. Birney, Gerrit Smith and others, who had ranked among its prominent supporters, shortly after withdrew from it. In 1833 the British

Parliament passed the act for the West India emancipation, and the result was a great impulse to the cause of anti-slavery in the United States.

But no more States could be induced to try emancipation. The anti-slaveryites formed societies, and raised the cry of "immediate abolition." They deluged Congress with petitions, and the country with tracts, pamphlets and newspapers. Thousands and millions of pages of printed matter were sent out, but all in vain. "Moral suasion" accomplished nothing, and "slavery" not only remained as firm as ever, but it had extended and fortified itself in such a manner that the Abolitionists themselves gave up their "immediate abolition" demand in utter despair. They cried, but no one listened. They expostulated, but the public heeded them not. The freed negroes of the North were a standing monument to the folly of Abolitionism. They had not progressed, or shown themselves active, enterprising members of society. They would black boots, whitewash and do other menial offices, and they would hold conventions and pass ridiculous resolutions, but as for clearing up land and settling themselves in independent circumstances, they would not. In 1852 Gerrit Smith, who has done more for freed blacks than any other man, for he gave all who would accept them, free homes on his lands, complained in a letter to Governor Hunt that "the most of them preferred *to rot both physically and morally* in cities, rather than become farmers or mechanics in the country." His own experiment with them resulted in signal failure. Even Horace Greeley, in a moment of apparent forgetfulness, declared in the *Tribune*, September 22, 1855, that "nine-tenths of the free blacks have no idea of setting themselves to work except as the hirelings or scrivers of white men ; no idea of building a church or other serious enterprise, except through beggary of the whites. *As a class, the blacks are indolent, improvident, servile and licentious.*"

We have shown what the condition of the freed negro population of the North was in 1826-'27, according to the statistics of the Boston Prison Discipline Society. We will now give some figures and facts from the United States Census Report of 1850, showing the number of black and white convicts in the penitentiaries of the four States of Massachusetts, New York, Pennsylvania and Ohio, and the proportion of free negro convicts over the whites :

POPULATION IN 1850.

	Mass.	N. Y.	Penn.	Ohio.
Whites	985.450	3,048,325	2,258,160	1,955,050
Free Negroes	9,084	49,069	53,626	25,279

NUMBER IN THE PENITENTIARIES AND STATE PRISONS.

	Mass.	N. Y.	Penn.	Ohio.
Whites	889	1,380	323	362
Free Negroes	47	257	109	44

It will be seen from the above, that in Massachusetts there was one white convict to every 2,533 of white population. In New York there was one white convict to every 2,208 of white population. In Pennsylvania one to every 6,884, and in Ohio one to every 5,400. But how stands the case as to the free negroes? Why, in Massachusetts, there was one free negro convict to every 192 of the free negro population. In New York one to every 190. In Pennsylvania one to every 492, and in Ohio one to every 574. It is instructive to note these facts. It appears that crime among the free negroes of Massachusetts is over *eight* times greater than among the white population. Yet the negroes of Massachusetts have enjoyed the benefits of "impartial freedom" ever since 1780. It would seem, therefore, that the more you try to force white man's rights upon them, the lower and lower they sink in the scale of morality.

The freed negro population of the United States has increased from 59,466 in 1790, to 434,495 in 1850, and 491,823 in 1860. In some States it has become so large as to excite well grounded alarm, and what is remarkable, some of the very States that have little or none of this population among them, are industriously engaged in trying to force it upon others. The six eastern States, as is shown by the census returns of 1850—Maine, New Hampshire, Vermont, Massachusetts, Rhode Island and Connecticut—have 65,440 square miles; and in 1850 they had 23,021 freed negroes in the six States. By the census taken in 1790 they had 17,042 free and slave. The State of New York has 46,220 square miles, and had 49,069 free negroes in 1850. She has to-day, under the census of 1860, 49,031—a decrease. The six New England States, and New York, have 111,660 square miles, and 72,090 free negroes. *The little State of Maryland, has but* 10,755 *square miles; and in* 1850 *she had* 74,723 *free negroes ; according to the census of* 1860 *she has nearly* 84,000! The State of Pennsylvania has 46,215 square miles, lying upon the northern border of the State of Maryland, only divided by an imaginary line, and who had 53,626 free negroes in 1850. Thus wo see that the State of Maryland has not one-fourth as many square miles as Pennsylvania, and yet Maryland has, by the census of 1860, 27,345 more free blacks than the State of Pennsylvania. The State of Delaware has, by the census of 1860, 19,723 free negroes. The District of Columbia has 11,107 free negroes, and if no slaves had been removed before the abolition of "slavery," this number would have been increased to 14,000—and this, too, is a territory less than ten miles square! Here, then, we see the comparatively small territory comprising the States of Maryland, Delaware and the District of Columbia, cursed with no less than 115,000 free negroes! Set free all their "slave" negro population, which previous to the emancipation in the District of Columbia must have been about 100,000, and there would be 215,000 free negroes on 13,000 square miles, or one negro to every 2½ white persons! No people can stand such an incubus of black laziness, vice and crime, as this state of affairs would produce, to say nothing of degrading the white population to a level with the negro. It will not be, it cannot be a long time before the cry, "Abolition of free negroism," will be raised in Maryland and Delaware, unless the people are deprived of all right of self-government. If allowed to go on, free negroism will yet produce a social convulsion in those States and elsewhere, to which even civil war, with all its horrors, will be but a faint parallel. Robespierre and Brissot, in 1791, tried the "impartial freedom" of Sumner and Greeley, in St. Domingo—and Alison has vividly painted the result.—Speaking of the Haytien tragedy, he says,— "That negroes *marched with spiked infants on their spears, instead of colors; then sawed asunder the male prisoners, and violated the females on the dead bodies of their husbands.*" The mind of white persons can scarcely conceive of such infernal atrocities, and yet they are common to negroes, when perverted into what is called freedom.

From all that has been presented, then, it is easy to see that the present condition of the freed negroes of the North is of the most degraded character, and after fifty years of freedom, they are worse instead of better off. They are engaged in no *productive* employments; they furnish a large proportion of our criminals; they fill up our alms houses; and hence are a constant tax upon while e labor. If their number according to the population was as great as it was when Massachusetts and Pennsylvania were complaining of the burden they cast upon them, our people would not stand the incubus it would be upon their labor and industry. The free negroes of the North do not now, owing to the immigration and the immense white population, form an appreciable element of society. If they did, our people would demand a remedy, even to a return of those negroes to the care and protection of persons, who would guarantee that they should not become public burdens. Society scarcely appreciates the burden of one negro living upon the industry of 100 white, as in Massachusetts, but when free negroes become as numerous as in Maryland, where there is one to every *five* whites, they become an intolerable weight, and must irretrievably drag down any State that submits to it.—The crimes and indolence of these people are not, however, so much to be charged to their account as to the whites, who, with sufficient intelligence to know and comprehend this race, and their duties towards it, shut their eyes from mere *party* spirit, to absolute facts, and keep on neglecting and persecuting it under the name of philanthropy. The effort to make the negro live out the life or manifest the capabilities of the white man, is just like trying to force the woman to live the life of a man, or a child to exhibit the capabilities of the adult, or an ox to perform the duties of a horse! Each one of God's creatures has his specific organization and his specific life, and it is just as reasonable to expect a white man to be an angel as it is to expect a negro to be a white man ; that is, to act as a white man, to think as a white man, or to work as a white man. Hence it is, as we have shown, that crime, disease and death mark the career of Free Negroism. It destroys the negro, drags down white men, burdens them with taxes, and must inevitably end, where the number of the two races approximate, in social convulsions and a horrible and revolting war of races.

PART II.

FREE NEGROISM ELSEWHERE.

Having taken a brief glance at free negroism among ourselves, we will now take a general survey of it elsewhere. Freeing the negro in temperate latitudes, where the number was limited, was a matter of no moment in its effect upon the interest of commerce or civilization. White labor, better adapted to those regions, rushed in to supply its place, and if no emancipation had occurred, the result would have been even more healthy, for the negro labor, rendered unprofitable, would have been sent southward, where it would have been productively employed in raising articles to be exchanged for the skilled labor of more northern latitudes. In order, therefore, to see the really disastrous effects of free negroism, we must turn our attention to that vast tropical territory, which has been cursed with this miserable delusion. Many people, perhaps, have no idea of the vast territory, which now lies an uncultivated waste, solely from the effects of removing the negro from the control of the superior race. The entire continent of North and South America, from the Rio Grande on the North to Brazil on the South, is, to day, little more than a desert waste. The devil of free negroism has done its work. But this is not all. Those beautiful and fertile islands—the West Indies—with the exception of Cuba and Porto Rico, are in the same condition. Let us see how much land is thus lying unproductive and neglected.

The number of square miles in the territory to which we have alluded, is as follows:—

	Square miles.
Mexico	829,916
Central America	155,770
Venezuela	426,712
New Granada	521,948
Ecuador	287,638
British Guiana	96,000
Dutch Guiana	59,765
French Guiana	22,500
West India Islands	150,000
Total	2,550,249

The United States and Territories comprise an area of 2,946,166 square miles, so that here is an extent of territory nearly equal to the entire length and breadth of our country, which, with here and there an exception, lies an unproductive waste. If the curse of God had rested upon it, and, like the Cities of the Plain, it had been covered with a bituminous lake, its condition would not be materially different. But, instead of that, so far as the Creator is concerned, it is the most glorious land the sun ever shone upon. Perpetual summer reigns, and the fertility of the soil is as exhaustless as the sea. The variety and extent of its productions are almost unbounded, but, as God said before He made Adam, "lo! there is no one to till the ground." The negro freed, basks in idleness, and only performs just sufficient labor to keep life in his lazy body. The earth, however, is so rich in spontaneous produc ions, that the labor which necessity requires, is comparatively none ; and hence Cuffee indulges his constitutional complaint of laziness to its full extent. It would require more space than we have at our disposal to give a review of the decrepitudo and decay of tho vast extent of territory from the Rio Grande to the Amazon. But a brief extract from Prof. Holton's work on "New Granada,"‡ will give an indication of it. Speaking of the Valley of the Cauca, in that country, he says :

"What more could nature do for this people, or what has she withholden from them ?   What production of any zone would be unattainable by patient industry, *if they knew of such a virtue ?*   But their valley seems to be enriched with the greatest fertility and tho finest climate in tho world, only to show the *miraculous power of idleness* and unthrift to keep land poor.   Here the family have sometimes *omited their dinner, just because there was nothing to eat in the house !*   Maize, cocoa, and rice, when out of season, can hard.y be had for love or money ; so this valley, a very Eden by nature, is filled with *hunger and poverty.*"

Now there are over 2,000,000 of square miles essentially in the same position—the inhabitants, degraded in morals, lazy in habits, and worthless in every respect. The improvements under tho Spaniards are gone to decay and ruin, while the mongrel population do nothing except insult the name of " God and Liberty" by indulging in pronunciamentos and revolutions!

THE WEST INDIA ISLANDS.

From these Islands, where emancipation was inaugurated as an example for us to follow, we propose to draw our principal illustrations of the failure of free negroism. This is the more important, because the anti-slaveryites still endeavor to cling to tho delusion that it has been a success, and try to palm off the statement upon the public for fact. The West India Islands comprise, it is estimated, in all about 150,000 square miles, or an extent of territory as large as the States of Georgia, Alabama and Mississippi. Some of the smaller islands are uninhabited, but those inhabited, and more or less under cultivation, have an area, as stated in Colton's Atlas, of 96,000 square miles. Cuba takes off 42,000 square miles, leaving 54,000 in Hayti and the British and French Islands. When emancipation took place in Jamaica, in 1834, it was loudly heralded that free labor in the West Indies would soon render "slavery" entirely unprofitable in the United States. Mr. Birney encouraged his followers with this hope, and Wm. Lloyd Garrison even made tho confident prediction that the "American slave system must inevitably perish from starvation." George Thompson, the English Abolitionist, who came over to this country about that time to fan the flame of anti-southern agitation, declared that " soon all slave labor cotton would be repu-

---

‡ New Granada : Twenty Months in the Andes. By Isaac F. Holton, M.A. Harper & Brothers.

diated by the English manufacturers." The labor of negroes was to accomplish all this, for it was presumed that freedom would give an impetue to production, and that the enterprise and industry of the freed black men would soon far outstrip the resources of those countries where "the unprofitable and expensive system of slave labor" was still adhered to. The millenium was thus, in 1833, but just a step ahead of the Abolitionists. They had almost clutched the El Dorado of negro perfection. But alas! for their confident anticipations and positive predictions. In six years the answer came, and it was as follows: In 1800 the West Indies exported 17,000,000 lbs. of cotton and the United States 17,789,803 lbs. They were thus at this timo about equally productive. In 1840 the West Indies exported only 866,157 lbs. of cotton, while the United States exported 743,941,061 lbs! Instead, therefore, of the "American system dying of starvation," as Garrison predicted, or of the British spinners refusing to use "slave" grown cotton, England went right on manufacturing "slave" grown cotton, while her "philanthropists," to keep up the delusion, began to talk about raising cotton in Africa, by free negro labor there, and they have kept on *talking* about it, and all the while *using* the productions of "slave" labor. But, in order to give the reader a fuller and more complete view of the terrible blow the industrial resources of the world have received by emancipation in the West India Ielands, we propose to take up a few of the more important Islands, and notice their decline with some minuteness. As it was the first to try "impartial freedom," we commence with

HAYTI.

This Island is divided into two parts—the western portion being Hayti proper, and the eastern forming the Dominican Republic. It is next in size to Cuba, and is regarded as the most fertile of the Antilles. The entire island is 406 miles in length by a maximum width of 163. The number of square miles is 27,690, of which 10,091 are comprised in the Haytien or negro Republic, and the balance in the Dominican. It is very difficult to arrive at the exact population of Hayti, as no definite statistics exist, but it is variously estimated at from 550,000 to 650,000. The climate, natural productions and fertility of its soil are not surpassed by any other portion of the known world. Gold, silver, platina, mercury, copper, iron, tin, sulphur, rock salt, jasper, marble, &c., &c., are found among its mineral productions. The gold mines have long since been abandoned, as has every employment requiring laborious industry. The climate is warm, but, on account of the sea breezes, generally agreeable and pleasant, even during the summer heats. Vegetation is of the richest and most luxuriant kind.

"It is extremely difficult," says a traveler, "to convey to one unacquainted with the richness and variety of the Island scenery of the tropics, a correct impression of its gorgeous beauty. Islands rising from a crystal sea, clothed with a vegetation of surpassing luxuriance and splendor, and of every variety, from the tall and graceful palm, the stately and spreading mahogany, to the bright flowers that seem to have stolen their tints from the glowing snn above them. Birds with colors as varied and gorgeous as the hues of the rainbow, flit amid the dark green foliage of the forests, and flamingoes, with their scarlet plumage, fla-h along the shore. Fish of the same varied hues glide through waters so clear that for fathoms below the surface they can be distinctly seen. Turn the oye where it will, on sea or land, some bright color flashes before it. Nature is here a queen indeed, and dressed for a gala day.

"In the island of St. Domingo, the rich beauty of the tropics is combined with some of the finest mountain scenery in the world. The broad, fertile lagoons, covered with groves of orange, citron and coffee, with here and there a delicate column of smoke indicating the locality of some invisible dwelling; groves of mangroves, rising apparently from the midst of the waters, but indicating the presence of dangerous shallows, gradually become visible. No rough promontory, as upon our northern shores, meets the eye; every angle is delicately rounded, every feature of the scenery undulating and graceful."

To this surpassing beauty is added almost all the natural productions that can be conceived. The mountains are covered with forests of pine, mahogany, fustic, satin wood, lignum vi're and other cabinet woods. All the usual tropical productions grow spontaneously in great abundance, including plantains, bananas, yams, maize, millet, oranges, pine apples, melons, grapes, &c. The staples of cultivation are coffee, cocoa, sugar, indigo, cotton and tobacco. Surely, such a country as this has been peculiarly blessed by the Creator, and it seems nothing less than a crime against nature to allow its exhaustless resources to remain undeveloped. But what is its history?

In 1790 Hayti was in a high state of prosperity. At that time it supplied half of Europe with sugar. It was a French colony, and contained a population which numbered about 500,000, of which 33,360 were whites and 28,370 free negroes, mostly mulattoes. The remainder were negro "slaves." The period of which we speak was the era of the great French Revolution, when the doctrines of "liberty, equality and fraternity" had full sway in France. The colonists or white people of Hayti entered with great fervor into the support of these doctrines, but they intended them to apply to white men, and *white men only*. But this did not suit the pleasure of the "Mountain Department" of the French Assembly. That demanded "impartial freedom," and "impartial freedom" it was. In 1793 the freedom of the blacks in Hayti was decreed, and the grand experiment of "impartial freedom" commenced. The result of that experiment is now, after seventy years' trial, before the world. If the negro has any capacity for self-government, any of the inherent, natural abilities or energies of the white man, surely he ought to have shown them during this time. With a country whose natural resources and fertility are beyond question, and with a climato exactly suited to the physical peculiarities of the race, surely there should have been no such word as fail. The island had been brought to a high state of cultivation, and to an exalted commercial prosperity by the French planters. It was turned over to its new masters like a garden ready cultivated, and all they had to do was to keep it as it was, and go on in the career of prosperity which had been so successfully inaugurated. But what are the facts? A few statistics will show, more vividly than words, how fearfully the island has retrograded, and how fallacious are all the hopes which have been indulged in, as to the industry of negroes, when left to themselves. In 1790 the value of the exports of Hayti were $27,828,000, the principal productions being as follows:

Sugar, lbs.	163,405,220
Coffee, do.	68,151,180
Cotton, do.	6,286,126
Indigo, do.	930,016

In 1826, about thirty years after emancipation, the figures stood thus:

Sugar, lbs.	32,864
Coffee, do.	32,189,784
Cotton, do.	620,972
Indigo, do.	none

Now there is no sugar at all exported, while coffee and logwood have become the principal items of export. The former is gathered wild from the mountains, or from the old abandoned, French plantations, while all that is required in order to get the latter, is to cut down the tree, which grows spontaneously, and take it to market. It is, therefore, seen that all *cultivation* is abandoned, and only those articles are now exported which require no labor to produce them. In 1849, the latest date of which we have any reliable statistics, and sixty years after emancipation, the exports of the articles we have named were as follows:—

Sugar, lbs.	none.
Coffee, lbs.	30,608,343
Cotton, lbs.	544,516
Indigo, lbs.	none.

It is impossible to state, with accuracy, what the present value of the exports of Hayti amount to. Mr. Sumner, in a recent speech in the Senate, placed them at $2,673,000. This, we apprehend, is just about double the real value. A recent traveler, Mr. Underhill, says he could find *no statistics* in Hayti as to her commerce, and Mr. Sumner's figures are, doubtless, mere guess work. But grant what Mr. Sumner says, and what a doleful picture of commercial ruin it presents! In 1790, the exports of Hayti amounted to $27,828,000, and now, according even to Abolition testimony, they foot up only $2,633,000! Comment is unnecessary.

The statistics we have quoted are taken from the "U. S. Commercial Relations," vol. I, pp. 531-2, officially reported to Congress, and published by order of that body. But all these figures are fully corroborated by every candid and impartial traveler. A foreign resident at the capital of Hayti, under a recent date, writes:—

"This country has made, since it's emancipation, no progress whatever. The population purially live upon the products of the grown wild coffee plantations, remnants of the French dominion. Properly speaking, plantations after the model of the English in Jamaica, or the Spanish in Cuba, do not exist here. Hayti is the most beautiful and the most fertile of the Antilles. It has more mountains than Cuba, and more space than Jamaica. Nowhere

the coffee tree could better thrive than here, as it especially likes a moun-
tainous soil. But the *indolence of the negro has brought the once splendid
plantations to decay.* They now gather coffee *only from the grown wild
trees.* The cultivation of the sugar cane has *entirely disappeared,* and
the island that once supplied the one-half of Europe with sugar, now sup-
plies its own wants from Jamaica and the United States."

In order to show the present condition of Hayti more fully, we quote from
a work just published in London, entitled "The West Indies—Their Moral
and Social Condition." The author, Mr. E. B. Underhill, was sent out by
the Baptist Missionary Society of London, and is an Abolitionist of the
deepest dye. While finding all the excuses he can for the decay of the
Island, he is forced to own the truth. He describes his journey to Port au
Prince as follows :

" We passed by many, or through *many abandoned plantations, the build-
ings in ruin,* the sugar mills decayed, *and the iron pans strewing the road-
side, cracked and broken.* But for the law that forbids, on pain of confisca-
tion, the export of all metals, they would long ago have been sold to foreign
merchants.

" Only once in this long ride did we come upon a mill in use ; it was grind-
ing cane, in order to manufacture the syrup from which *tofia* is made, a
kind of inferior rum, the intoxicating drink of the country. The mill was
worked by a large over-shot or water-wheel, the water being brought by an
aqueduct from a very considerable distance. With the exception of a few
banana gardens, or small patches of maize round the cottages, no where
did this magnificent and fertile plain show signs of cultivation.

"In the time of the French occupation, before the Revolution of 1793,
thousands of hogsheads of sugar were produced; *now, not one. All is decay
and desolation.* The pastures are deserted, and the prickly pear covers the
land once laughing with the bright hues of the sugar cane.

"The hydraulic works, erected at vast expense for irrigation, *hove crum-
bled to dust. The plow is an unknown implement of culture,* although so
eminently adapted to the great plains and deep soil of Hayti.

" A country, so capable of producing for export, and therefore for the
enrichment of its people—besides sugar, and coffee, cotton, tobacco, the
cacao bean, spices, every tropical fruit, and many of the fruits of Europe—
lies uncultivated, unoccupied and desolate. Its rich mines are neither ex-
plored nor worked ; and its beautiful woods rot in the soil where they grow.
A little log wood is exported, but ebony, mahogany and the finest building
timber rarely fall before the woodman's axe, and then only for local use.
The present inhabitants despise *all servile labor,* and are, for the most part,
content with *the spontaneous productions of the soil and forest.*"

The degraded, barbarous condition of the negroes of Hayti, is well illustrated in a description given by Mr. Underhill, of what is known as "the
religion of Vaudoux, or serpent worship." It is a native African supersti-
tion, and proves, beyond all question, the rapid return of the Hayti negroes
to the original savagism of their African ancestors. Mr. U. gives a full description of the ceremonies of this heathenish rite, as described to him by
one of the resident missionaries, which we regret we have not space to give
entire. The performances are preceded by the following barbaric chorus :

" Eh ! eh ! Bomba, hen ! hen !
Canga bafio to
Canga mourno do le
Canga de ki li
Canga li."

The object worshipped *is a small green snake,* and the custom is a purely

African heathenism. The negro always has a predisposition to it, but it is repressed when he is under white control. Of late years it has been revived extensively in Hayti.

"The Vaudoux," says Mr. Underhill, "meet in a retired spot, designated at a previous meeting. On entering they take off their shoes, and bind about their bodies handkerchiefs, in which a red color predominates. The king is known by the scarlet band around his head, worn like a crown, and a scarf of the same color distinguishes the queen. The object of adoration, the serpent, is placed on a stand. It is then worshipped; after which the box is placed on the ground, the queen mounts upon it, is seized with violent tremblings, and gives utterance to oracles in response to the prayers of the worshippers. A dance closes the ceremony. The king puts his hand on the serpent's box; a tremor seizes him, which is communicated to the circle. A delirious whirl or dance ensues, heightened by the free use of tafia. The weakest fall, as if dead, upon the spot. The bachanalian revellers, always dancing and turning about, are borne away into a place near at hand, where sometimes under the triple excitement of *promiscuous intercourse*, drunkenness and darkness, scenes are enacted, enough to make the impassible gods of Africa itself gnash their teeth with horror."

What a disgusting picture of savagism and heathenism does not this present! And yet, there are people who try to palm off upon the world the idea that negroes can remain civilized when left to themselves. This same missionary, Mr. Webley, writing to the London *Missionary Herald*, in 1850, says: "These Vaudoux almost deluge the Haytien part of the Island. They practice witchcraft and mysticism to an almost indefinite extent. They are singular *adepts at poisoning*. A person rarely escapes them when *he has been fixed upon as a victim*." It is thus seen that Obeism is quite as prevalent in Hayti as it is in the interior of Africa. What more need be said to prove the relapse of these negroes into their original barbarism? Such, then, is the condition of Hayti. Production gone, commerce gone, and the negroes themselves returning to their original African heathenism !

JAMAICA.

Jamaica is about 150 miles long by about 50 in width. Its area is about 6,400 square miles, or 4,000,000 of acres. It is the largest and most valuable of the British West India Islands. The last census taken was in 1844, when the population stood as follows:—Whites, 15,776 ; negroes, 293,128 ; mulattoes, 68,529. By the census of 1861, the only one taken since, the population is stated as follows:— Whites, 13,816; mulattoes, 81,065; negroes, 346,374. The whole number of persons who can read is set down at 80,724, and 50,726 as able to read and write. It will be seen from this that over 300,000 can neither read nor write. The education is evidently confined to the whites and mulattoes, leaving the negroes in their natural ignorance, where they have neither oral nor any other instruction. Of course "educated," negroes are simply monstrosities, but as some people seem to suppose that "freedom" will develop such "white crows," we have cited these statistics to show that Jamaica has not yet produced them, after a twenty-five years' trial. The white population, it will also be seen, is gradually decreasing—dying out—through the blood of the negro.

The productions of Jamaica are similar to those of the other West India Islands. The soil is deep and fertile, and one of the best in the world for the production of sugar, coffee, pimento and ginger. It is also rich in minerals, cabinet woods, &c., and the low grounds yield abundantly the plantain, banana, yam, sweet potatoes, pine apples, oranges, pomegranates, &c, &c. Jamaica has been in possession of England ever since the days of Oliver Cromwell, and at the time of the prohibition of the importation of negroes from Africa in 1807, was in a most flourishing condition. Her history, since then, has been one of gradual but sure decay. The restriction upon her supply of labor produced some decrease in her productions, and the abolition of "slavery" in 1833 hastened the final destruction of the Island. The negroes freed in 1833 were to serve five years as apprentices, and on the 1st of August, 1838, to have their unconditional liberty. For this injury to the negro and crime towards the white man, the planters were allowed about $30,000,000, the whole sum expended in all the Islands, by the British government, being about $100,000,000. And what is the result? Facts speak louder than words, and to them we appeal. The value of the exports of Jamaica (we quote from the Cyclopedia of Commerce, published by Harper & Brothers, of this city,) before and after the emancipation, will illustrate what we say :—

BEFORE EMANCIPATION.

Years.	Value of Exports.
1809	£3,033,234
1810	2,303,579

AFTER EMANCIPATION.

1853	£937,276
1854	932,316

The productions of Jamaica show, forcibly, what the above figures exhibit by values. In 1805, two years before the prohibition of African emigration, the productions of Jamaica were as follows :

PRODUCTS OF JAMAICA IN 1805.

Sugar	150,352 hhds.
Rum	46,837 punch.
Pimento	1,041,540 lbs.
Coffee	17,961,923 lbs.

The production of the island, at that time, was at its highest point. The sugar was the largest crop ever produced in Jamaica. The loss of labor was severely felt, especially in the sugar culture, so that in 1834, the year emancipation was effected, the production stood as follows :

PRODUCTS OF JAMAICA IN 1834.

Sugar	84,756 ht.ds.
Rum	32,111 punch.
Pimento	3,605,400 lbs.
Coffee	17,725,731 lbs.

In the very next year, the first one under free negroism, there was a manifest falling off. The sugar production was only 77,970 hhds., nearly 10,000 hhds. less ; coffee was only 10,503,018 lbs., a decrease of over 7,000,000 lbs., and this decrease has steadily continued, until in 1856 the production of Jamaica stood as follows :

PRODUCTS OF JAMAICA IN 1856.

Sugar	25,920 bhds.
Rum	14 470 punch.
Pimento	6,848,622 lbs.
Coffee	3,328,147 lbs.

The only crop that had increased was that of pimento, or allspice, the increase of which, instead of being an evidence of the industry of the negro, is the reverse. The pimento tree grows wild in Jamaica, and rapidly spreads over land formerly under cultivation. As the plantations were abandoned, they were overrun with this tree, and the negro women and children picked the berries without the trouble of cultivation. The coffee tree, to a certain extent, is like the pimento, and grows wild in many places. Hence the production of coffee has not fallen off in the same proportion as that of sugar, which can only to produced by careful cultivation. The coffee crop of Jamaica, however, was in 1813, before the overthrow of "slave" labor, 34,045,585 lbs., but the average crop for the past ten years has not been over 5,000,000 lbs., while the sugar crop had fallen in 1853 as low as 20,000 hhds! These facts and statistics demonstrate the down-hill progress of Jamaica, and show what may be expected wherever the experiment of free negroism is attempted.

The rapidity with which estates have been abandoned in Jamaica, and the decrease in the taxable property of the Island, is also astounding. The movable and immovable property of Jamaica was once estimated at £50,000,000, or nearly $250,000,000. In 1850 the sees od valuation had fallen to £11,500,000. In 1351 it was reduced to £9,500,000, and Mr. Westmoreland, in a speech in the Jamaica House of Assembly, stated it was believed, that the falling off would be £2,000,000 more in 1852. From a report made to the House of Assembly of the number and extent of the plantations abandoned during the years 1848, '49, '50, '51 and '52, we gather the following facts :—

Sugar estates abandoned	128
" partially "	71
Coffee plantations abandoned	96
" partially "	66

The total number of acres thus thrown out of cultivation in five years was 391,187! This is only a sample, for the same process has been going on ever since emancipation. In the five years immediately succeeding emancipation, the abandoned estates stood as follows :—

Sugar estates 140	168,032 acres.
Coffee plantations 465	188,400 acres.

These plantations employed 40,383 laborers, whose industry was, therefore, at once lost to the world, and the articles they had raised were just so much subtracted from consumption. The price of these articles, sugar and coffee, was increased on account of the diminished production, and that increased cost represented the tax which the world paid for the privilege of allowing Sambo to loll in idleness. The Cyclopedia of Commerce says "that *the negro is rapidly receding into a savage state*, and that unless there is a large and immediate supply of immigrants, *all society will come to a speedy end*, and the island become a second Hayti."

Such, then, is the condition of Jamaica, as stated in an impartial work. Let us hear now what the London *Times* candidly owns up to. I. says :

"There is *no blinking the truth*. Years of bitter experience, years of hope deferred, of self-devotion unrequited, of prayers unanswered, of sufferings derided, of insults unresented, of contumely patiently endured, have convinced us of the truth. It must be spoken out loudly and energetically, despite the wild mockings of 'howling cant.' *The freed West India slave will not till the soil for wages ;* the free son of the ex-slave is as obstinate as his sire. He will not cultivate lands which he has not bought for his own. Yams, mangoes and plantains—these satisfy his wants ; he cares not for yours. Cotton, sugar, coffee and tobacco he cares but little for. And what matters it to him that the Englishman has sunk his thousands and tens of thousands on mills, machinery and plants, which now totter on the languishing estate, that for years has only returned him beggary and debt. He eats his yams and sniggers at 'Buckra.' We know not why this should be, but so it is. The negro has been bought with a price—the price of English *taxation* and English *toil*. He has been redeemed from bondage *by the sweat and travail of some millions of hard-working Englishmen*. Twenty millions of pounds sterling—one hundred millions of dollars—have been *distilled from the brains and muscles of the free English laborer*, of every degree, to fashion the West India negro into a 'free, independent laborer.' 'Free and independent' enough he has become, God knows, but laborer he *is not ;* and, so far as we can see, *never will be*. He will sing hymns and quote texts, but honest, steady industry he not only detests but *despises*."

Such is the testimony of the London *Times*—such the universal evidence of every candid individual. How different is this picture from that predicted by the Abolitionists ! The Rev. Dr. Channing, the Dr. Cheever of that day, made the following prophecy in 1833, as the result of emancipation :—

"The planters, in general, would suffer little, if at all, from emancipation. This change would make them *richer* rather than poorer. One would think, indeed, from the common language on the subject, that the negroes were to be annihilated by being set free ; that the whole labor of the South was to be destroyed by a single blow. But the colored man, when freed, will not vanish from the soil. He will stand there with the same muscles as before, only strung anew by liberty ; with the same limbs to toil, and with *stronger motives* to toil than before. He will work from *hope*, not fear ; will work for himself, not for others ; and unless all the principles of human nature are reversed under a black skin, he will work *better than before*. We believe that agriculture will revive, our worn-out soils will be renewed, and the whole country assume a brighter aspect under *free labor*."

This is the same story the Abolitionists are singing now, not having yet learned that "the principles of human nature are reversed under a black skin"—that is, of *white* human nature, and it was from a total misconception of the negro that Dr. Channing fell into his grand mistake. Mr. Anthony Trollope, an Englishman, and an anti-slavery man, who has written a book on Jamaica, seems to know rather more of the negro race than Dr. Channing did. The London *Times*, drawing its facts from Mr. Trollope, says of it :

"A servile race, peculiarly fitted by nature for the hardest physical work in a burning climate. The negro has no desire for property strong enough to induce him to labor with sustained power. He lives from hand to month. In order that he may have his dinner, and some small finery, he will work a little, but after that he is content to *l'ein the sun*. This, in Jamaica, he can very easily do, for emancipation and free trade have combined to throw enormous tracts of land out of cultivation, and on these the negro squats, getting all that he wants with very little trouble, and sinking, in the most resolute fashion, to the savage state. Lying under his cotton-tree, he refuses to work after ten o'clock in the morning. 'No, tar kee, massa, me tired now; me no want more money.' Or, by the way of variety, he may say :— 'No, workee no more; money no nuff; workee no pay.' And so the planter must see his canes foul with weeds, because he cannot prevail on Sambo to earn a second shilling by going into the cane fields. He calls him a lazy nigger, and threatens him with starvation. His answer is: 'No, massa; no starve now; God send plenty yam.' These yams, be it observed, on which Sambo lives, and on the strength of which he declines to work, are grown on the planter's own ground, and probably planted at his own expense. "There lies the shiny, oily, odorous negro, under his mango-tree, eating the luscious fruit in the sun. He sends his black urchin up for a bread-fruit, and, behold, the family table is spread. He pierces a cocoa-nut, and lo! there is his beverage. He lies on the ground, surrounded by oranges, bananas, and pine-apples. Why should he work? Let Sambo himself reply : 'No, massa, me weak in mo belly; me no workee to-day; me no like workee just um little moment.' "

This is a graphic description of the negro character, where the climate gives him a chance to show out his real nature. The same author says that "one-half of the sugar estates, and *more than* one-half of the coffee plantations have gone back *into a state of bush*."

The idea of working for pay never entered in black nature. As long ago as Mungo Park traveled in Africa, he discovered that "paid servants, persons of free condition, voluntarily working for pay, *are unknown here*." No traveler in Africa, down to Dr. Livingston, has reversed that judgment.

In Lewis's West Indies, written 17 years before emancipation, it is remarked : "As to free blacks, they are unfortunately lazy and improvident ; most of them half starved, and only anxious to live from hand to mouth." Even those who profess to be tailors, carpenters, or coopers, are, for the most part, careless, drunken and dissipated, and never take pains sufficient to attain to any dexterity in their trades ! *As for a free negro hiring himself out for plantation labor, no instance of such a thing was ever known in Jamaica.*" Earl Grey said, in the House of Lords, on June 10, 1852, "that it was established by statistical facts that the negroes were *idle, and falling back in civilization ;* that, relieved from the coercion to which they were formerly subjected, and a couple of days' labor giving them enough food for a fortnight, the climate rendering clothing and fuel not necessary to life, they had no earthly motive to give a greater amount of service than for mere subsistence." Sir H. Light and Gov. Barkley have both shown, also, that the majority of the free negroes of the West Indies are living in idleness, and the French colonies, according to a work from M. Vacherot, published a few years ago at Paris, demonstrate the same ruinous result under their emancipation act.

Captain Hamilton, on his examination as a witness, before a select committee of Parliament, stated that "*Jamaica, without any exaggeration, had become a desert.*"

In 1850 Mr. John Bigelow, then one of the editors of the New York *Evening Post*, paid a visit to Jamaica, and wrote a book thereon. As the testimony of an anti-slavery man, his statements are given. Mr. Bigelow says that the land of that island is as prolific as any in the world. It can be bought for $5 to $10 per acre, and five acres confer the right of voting and eligibility to public offices. Planters offer $1 50 per day for labor ; 16 days' labor will enable a negro to buy land enough to make him a voter, and the market of Kingston offers a great demand for vegetables at all times. These facts, said Mr. Bigelow, place independence within the reach of every black. But what are the results ? There has been no increase in voters in 20 years. Lands run wild. Kingston gets its vegetables from the United States.

But we will accumulate proof—pile it up, if needed. Mr. Robert Baird, who is an enthusiastic advocate of "the glorious Act of British Emancipation," on visiting the West Indies for his health, could not fail to be struck with the desolate appearance there.

"That the West Indians," says Mr. Baird, "are always grumbling, is an observation often heard, and, no doub', it is very true that they are so. But let any one who thinks that the extent and clamor of the complaint exceeds the magnitude of the distress which has called it forth, go to the West Indies and judge for himself. Let him see with his own eyes THE NEGLECTED AND ABANDONED ESTATES—THE UNCULTIVATED FIELDS, FAST HURRYING BACK INTO A STATE OF NATURE, WITH ALL THE SPEED OF TROPICAL LUXURIANCE—THE DISMANTLED AND SILENT MACHINERY, THE CRUMBLING WALLS, AND DESERTED MANSIONS, WHICH ARE FAMILIAR SIGHTS IN MOST OF THE BRITISH WEST INDIAN COLONIES Let him then transport himself to the Spanish islands of Porto Rico and Cuba, and witness the life and activity which in these slave colonies prevail. Let him observe for himself the activity of the slaves—the improvements daily making in the cultivation of the fields and in the processes carried on at the Ingenois or sugar mills —and *the general, indescribable air of thriving and prosperity which surrounds the whole*—and then let him come back to England and say, if he honestly can, that the British West Indian planters and proprietors are grumblers, who complain without adequate cause."

Ex-Governor Wood, of Ohio, who paid a visit to Jamaica in 1853, and who is no friend to "slavery," says :—

"Since the blacks have been liberated, they have become indolent, insolent, degraded and dishonest. They are a rude, beastly set of vagabonds, lying naked under the streets, as filthy as the Hottentots, and I believe worse. On getting to the wharf of Kingston, the first thing the blacks of *both sexes, perfectly naked*, come swarming about the boat, and would dive for small pieces of coin that were thrown by the passengers. On entering the city the stranger is annoyed to death by black beggars at every step, and you must often show him your pistol or an uplifted cane to rid yourself of their importunities."

Sewell, in his work on the "Ordeal of Free Labor," in which he defends emancipation, and pleads for still more extended privileges to the blacks, says of Kingston :

"There is not a house in decent repair ; not a wharf in good order ; no pavement. no sidewalk, no drainages, and scanty water ; no light. There is nothing like work done. Wreck and ruin, destitution and neglect. The inhabitants, taken *en masse*, are steeped to the eyelids in immorality. The population shews unnatural decrease. Illegitimacy exceeds legitimacy. Nothing is replaced that time destroys. If a brick tumbles from a house to the street, it remains there. If a spout is loosened by the wind, it hangs by a thread till it falls ; if furniture is accidentally broken, the idea of having it mended is not entertained. A God-forsaken place, without life or energy, old, dilapidated, sickly, filthy, cast away from the anchorage of sound morality, of reason and of common sense. Yet this wretched hulk is the capital of an island the most fertile in the world. It is blessed with a climate the most glorious ; it lies rotting in the shadow of mountains that can be cultivated from summit to base with every produce of tropic and temperate region. It is the mistress of a harbor wherein a thousand line-of-battle ships can ride safely at anchor."

We might fill a volume with such quotations, showing the steady decline of the Island. But it is well to note the moral condition of the negro. The *American Missionary Association* is the strongest kind of Abolition testimony in regard to the moral condition of the negroes. The *American Missionary*, a monthly paper, and organ of the Association, for July, 1855, has the following quotation from the letters of one of the missionaries :—

"*A man here may be a drunkard, a liar, a Sabbath breaker, a profane man, a fornicator, an adulterer, and such like—and be known to be such— and go to chapel and hold up his head there, and feel no disgrace from these things*, because they are so common as to create a public sentiment in his favor. He may go to the communion table and cherish a hope of heaven, and not have his hope disturbed. I might tell of persons, guilty of some, if not all of these things, ministering in holy things."

The Report of the American and Foreign Anti-Slavery Society, for 1853, p. 170, says of the negroes,

"Their moral condition is very far from being what it ought to be. It is exceedingly dark and distressing. *Licentiousness prevails to a most alarming extent among the people.* * * * * The almost universal prevalence of intemperance is another prolific source of the moral darkness and degradation of the people. The great mass among all classes of the inhabitants, from the governor in his palace to the peasant in his hut—from the bishop in his gown to the beggar in his rags—are *all slaves to their cups.*"

So much for " freedom" elevating the blacks. It is complained that the marriage relation is not always regarded where " slavery" exists, but it would seem, from this statement, that " slavery" had done more for the moral improvement of the negro, in this respect, than he was at all disposed to do for himself.

Mr. Underhill endorses the stories "of the crowds of bastard children" in the Island, and says it is " too true." "Outside the nonconformist communities," he says, " neglect of marriage *is almost universal.* One clergyman informed me that of seventeen infants brought to his church for baptism, *fifteen*, at least, would be of illegitimate origin." In fact, from all the admissions made, it does not appear that there is any more marriage in Jamaica than in Africa. The churches, Mr. Underhill allows, are less attended than formerly, and there is evidently little of the religious training of the whites left among the people. The negro, however, has all the advantages of " impartial freedom," and "the highest offices of the S ate are open to colored men. They are found," says Mr. U., "in the Assembly,

in the executive, on the bench and at the bar. All colors mix freely."
This would be the paradise for Seward, Phillips and Greeley. Mr. Underhill
estimates the annual loss of wages to the people, from the decay of estates
and plantations, cannot be less than £300,000, or nearly $1,500,000! Ne-
groes who work at all, cannot be prevailed upon to do so, generally, more
than four days in the week, and rarely five. Mr. U. also states that it has
been officially ascertained that *two-thirds* of the persons employed on sugar
estates are *women and children*. Yet, notwithstanding all these facts, the
anti-slaveryito still adheres to his favorite hobby. He has excuses and pal-
liatives for his friend, the negro. True, Jamaica is ruined, but still emancipation is a success. The seasons are poor, the estates were mortgaged,
the planters have not treated the blacks kindly, and they have bought patches
of ground of their own rather than labor for others. Such are some of
the excuses of the friends of Sambo. But the facts still stand out in bold
relief, despite the assertion of "negro missionaries," who are interested in
keeping up the delusion. The *facts* they do admit. They cannot deny or
controvert them. This is all we ask—we need none of their excuses. In
order to relieve themselves of the odium of having ruined the fairest Island
of the Antilles, they would naturally look for reasons not chargeable to
them. But figures do not lie. The exports of Jamaica have been gradually decreasing ever since "slavery" in the Island was interfered with,
until they have dwindled down to insignificance, and, as theLondon *Times*
says, "there is no blinking the truth—the negroes will not work for wages,"
and hence the tropics are going back to jungle and bush, while white men
are taxed double the price they ought to be for all tropical products.

THE OTHER ISLANDS.

The careful survey we have taken of the condition of Jamaica, derived
both from official statistics and the evidences of anti-slavery men, render
it almost unnecessary to notice the remaining islands where emancipation
has been carried out. The story of Jamaica is the story of all. We will,
however, briefly notice the condition of Trinidad and Barbadoes, for these
islands are often held up by the discomfited Abolitionists as an evidence of
the success of emancipation. Again we will take their own evidence to van-
quish them. Trinidad contains 2020 square miles. Her soil is as fertile as
any of the islands, and if production has somewhat increased within the past
few years, it is owing entirely to the Coolie slave trade.

As illustrating the terrible ordeal through which Trinidad has passed, we
quote from Mr. Underhill. He says:—

"Three years after emancipation, in 1841, the condition of the island was
most deplorable; the laborers had, for the most part, abandoned the estates,
and taken possession of plots of vacant land, especially in the vicinity of
the towns, without purchase or lawful right. Vagrancy had become an
alarming habit of great numbers; every attempt to take a census of the
population was baffled by the frequent migrations which took place. Criminals easily evaded justice by absconding to places where they were unknown,

or by hiding themselves in the dense forests which in all parts edged so closely on the cleared lands. Drunkenness increased to an enormous degree, assisted by planters who freely supplied rum to the laborers, to induce them to remain as cultivators on their estates. High wages were obtained, only to be squandered in amusement, revelry and dissipation; at the same time, these high wages induced a diminished cultivation of food, and a corresponding increase in price and in the import of provisions from the neighboring islands and continent. The laborers steadily refused to enter into any contracts which would oblige them to remain in the service of a master; this would too much have resembled the state of slavery from which they had but just emerged. It was with reference to this state of things that Lord Harris wrote in 1848 :—'Liberty has been given to a heterogeneous mass of individuals, who can only comprehend license; a partition in the rights and privileges, and duties of civilized society has been granted to them; they are only capable of enjoying its vices.' "

With the help of Vagrant Acts and other legislative enactments, somewhat like order was established; and the introduction of Coolie labor has enabled Trinidad to recover from the state of poverty into which it has been plunged. The island, however, has been compelled to burden itself with a debt of $725,000 on account of the expenses of the Coolie slave trade, which is disguised under the name of apprenticeship.

According to Lord Harris, one-fourth of the entire negro population of Trinidad, in 1850, were living in idleness. Estates were wholly abandoned, and poverty stalked abroad. The Coolie labor arrested this downward tendency. Between 1847 and 1856, 47,739 Coolies were introduced into the West India possessions of Great Britain, the greater portion going to Trinidad and Guiana. These 47,739 protests against the idleness of the negro have about doubled the production of sugar in Trinidad—raising it from 20,000 to 40,000 hogsheads. But no thanks to the negro for this. It is none of his doings. Mr. Underhill declares that NOT ONE-FOURTH of the persons employed on the estates are negroes. Hence this increase in the sugar production of Trinidad is no evidence of the benefit of emancipation, but just the reverse.

The case of Barbadoes is still more emphatic, though the Abolitionists are never tired of referring to that island as the proof positive of the success of "free negro labor." Now, what is Barbadoes? Well, it is a small island, about large enough for a good sized water melon patch. It is about 21 miles long by 14 wide, and contains 100,000 acres of land, all told. It has 150,000 inhabitants, and is more thickly settled than China. There is not an acre of wild or unimproved land; not room, as Trollope says, "for a pic-nic." This land is monopolized by the whites; and, under a rigid system of vagrant laws, the black is compelled to work. If an idle negro is seen, he is set to work, at wages, or else compelled to DRAG A BALL AND CHAIN on the highways. Mr. Trollope says, "When emancipation came, there was no squatting ground for the poor Barbadian. He had still to work and make sugar—work quite as hard as he had done while yet a slave. He had to do that or to starve. Consequently, labor has been abundant in this island only." Now, how this "capsizes" all the stuff the anti-slavery-ites tell us about Barbadoes? Not long since there appeared in the *Inde-*

pendent, of this city, an article glorifying emancipation as it had affected
Barbadoes. Gov. Hincks, of that island, published a letter in proof of it, and
in it occurs this remarkable admission :—

"In Barbadoes, I have explained already that wages have ranged from
10l. to 1s. per task, and that rate prevails generally. In addition to these
wages, a small allotment of land is usually given, but on a most uncertain
tenure. The laborer may be EJECTED AT ANY TIME ON A FEW DAYS' NOTICE,
and no is subjected to PENALTIES FOR NOT WORKING ON THE ESTATE."

There is tho alternative to the negro, "work or starve." Does any one
suppose that the negroes of Barbadoes would work any better than the negroes of Jamaica, if there were plenty of unoccupied land in that island, as
there is in Jamaica, on which they could squat? If the negroes of Barbadoes are as enterprising as the Abolitionists would have us believe, why
do they not emigrate to Jamaica, where labor is in such demand, much
higher than in Barbadoes, and where land is plenty? The truth is easily
told. The negro never emigrates voluntarily anywhere. He works when
compelled to, and riots in idleness wherever he has a chance to show out
his nature. It is doubtful, however, whether the production of sugar in
Barbadoes is any larger now than it was nearly 200 years ago. It was one
of the first islands in which the Spaniards cultivated sugar, and in 1676
the sugar trade of Barbadoes required 400 vessels, of 150 tons each.* The
production of sugar in 1852 was 43,000 hogsheads. In 1836, the tonnage of
its shipping was 62,000, about tho same as in 1676. It is, therefore, quite
evident that thero has not been a material change in Barbadoee for many
years. The negroes have simply exchanged masters, and are probably
now in a worse condition than under the old system.

We have thus traced, with some minuteness, the present condition of four
of the principal West India Islands. Hayti, where the negro has been left
mainly to himself, we have seen, has gone back to its original, uncultivated
wilderness, and the inhabitants are sunk into the SAVAGEISM OF THEIR
AFRICAN ANCESTORS. They are rapidly losing even all conceptions of civilization, and, as soon as the mulattoes die out, the process will be complete. Abolitionism will have reared an African heathenism on this continent as the culmination of their bastard philanthropy. Civilization, and
all the wants of civilization, are utterly ignored by the negroes of Hayti.
The cotton, sugar, coffee, indigo, &c., which they ought to supply the
world, are left uncultivated.

Jamaica, the principal British West India island, though the white population there has struggled against it, presents essentially the same features.
Everywhere are desolation and ruin. These beautiful and fertile islands,
perfect "gems of the sea," are turned over to savageism, and ruined upon
the false and visionary idea that negroes are white men!

To present at a glance the effects of Free Negroism in the West India
Islands, and to sum up the whole subject in a brief space, it is only necessary to

---

* Sugar : Its Culture and Consumption. By P. L. Simmonds, of London.

examine the following table, showing the deficit in production under " free negro labor":

CONTRAST OF "SLAVE" NEGRO LABOR AND "FREE" NEGRO LABOR EXPORTS FROM THE WEST INDIES.

"SLAVE" NEGRO LABOR.			
	Years.	lbs. Sugar.	lbs. Coffee.	lbs. Cotton.
British West Indies	1807	636,025,643	31,610,764	17,000,000*
Hayti	1790	163,318,810	76,885,219	7,286,126
Total		809,344,453	108,245,988	24,286,126

"FREE" NEGRO LABOR.			
	Years.	lbs. Sugar.	lbs. Coffee.	lbs. Cotton.
British West Indies	1848	318,806,112	6,770,792	427.529†
Hayti	1848	very little.	34,114,717‡	1,591,454‡
Total		318,806,112	40,885,509	2,018,983
" Free " Negro Labor Deficit		490,088,341	67,300,474	22,207,143

If it were necessary to add to the proof we have given, that it is the overthrow of the supremacy of the white race, and that alone, that has produced this deplorable result, it is only required to cite the case of Cuba. Let Mr. Underhill, the British Abolitionst, from whom we have quoted, describe the difference between Cuba, where "slavery" exists, and where it does not. Of Havana he says :

"It is the BUSIEST AND MOST PROSPEROUS OF ALL THE CITIES OF the Antilles. Its harbor is one of the finest in the world, and IS CROWDED WITH SHIPPING. Its wharves and warehouses are piled with merchandize, and the general aspect is one of GREAT COMMERCIAL ACTIVITY. Its exoorts nearly reach the annual value of NINE MILLIONS STERLING, ($45,000,000,) and the customs furnish an annual tribute to the mother country over and above the cost of government and military occupation. EIGHT THOUSAND ships annually resort to the harbor of Cuba."

Evidently Mr. Underhill had got into a new world. He saw it, and was struck with the contrast it presented to the dilapidated region he had just left. In order to show the contrast between the PROGRESS of Cuba, and the DECLINE of Jamaica, it is only necessary to give a few statistics. The value of the exports of Jamaica, in 1809, were greater than those of Cuba in 1826, and a comparison of the two islands gives the following :—

Jamaica, in 1809	$15,166,000
Cuba, in 1826	13,809,388
Jamaica, in 1854	4,480 661
Cuba, in 1854	31,683,731

What a picture is this of free negroism! What can the Abolitionist, who prates of free negroes laboring, say to these facts and figures ? Cuba has been just as steadily advancing as Jamaica has been retrograding.

The productiveness of Cuba is most astonishing. Her exports are *more per head than those of any other country on the face of the globe.* Her export and import trade for 1859, was as follows : §

---

* 1800.   † 1840.   ‡ 1847.

§ Balanza General Del Commercio de la Isla de Cuba en 1859. Habana : 1861.

```
Exports for 1859..........................................$57,455,185
Imports for 1859..........................................  43,465,185
```

Showing an excess of exports over imports of............$13,989,506

Now, the population of Cuba is only about one million and a half, all told, black and white. Upon analysing the above figures, then, it will be seen that the exports of Cuba amount to about $40 per head for each man, woman and child on the island! At the same time, it should be noted that this great production is not all exchanged for articles imported, but there is a net income or surplus of exports over imports of $13,989,506.

This net surplus of wealth amounts to $9 32 cents for each man, woman and child in Cuba. No other country in the world can present such a picture of prosperity, and yet Cuba is by no means as productive as she might be. Through a mistaken policy, or supposed kindness to the negro, manumissions are easily procured and freed negroes are multiplying so rapidly that her welfare will, ere long, be very seriously impaired, unless the evil be checked.

But it will be instructive to take a glance at our own exports and imports, so that we may be able to see how much we are dependent upon negro labor for our prosperity. The exports of the fiscal year ending June 30th, 1860, embracing specie and American produce, amounted to $373,167,461 ; in addition to which we also re-exported about $27,000,000 of foreign produce, the result standing as follows :—

```
Exports for 1859-'60.... ......................$400,167,465
Imports for  "   " ..........................  361,727,209
```

Excess of exports over imports................:.$38,870,252

This gives a net surplus of only $1 26 cents per capita, while in Cuba, an exclusively negro labor country, it is $9 32 per head. Taking our *aggregate* domestic exports, and making a similar comparison, we find, calling our population in round numbers, thirty millions, that our exports per head are $12 43, against $40 per capita in Cuba.

Having shown now that the exports of the United States, North, South and West amount, we will call it, to $12½ per head, it will be interesting to *analyze* these exports and see where they come from. To whom is the country mainly indebted for this surplus wealth, which enables us to buy and pay for nearly four hundred millions of foreign goods per year ? It is very certain that we can have no imports, unless we have something to pay for them. Nor can we have any commerce unless we have something to sell which other nations want. It has been shown that the specie and American produce exported were, as above stated..................$373,167,461

Of this amount the specie was............................ 56,946,851

The amount of American produce consequently exported was..316,220,610

We propose to classify the amount furnished exclusively by the free States, the amount furnished by both the free and "slave" States, (which it is impossible to separate and designate the respective amount furnished by each,) and the amount furnished exclusively by the "slave" States.

FREE STATES EXCLUSIVELY :

Fisheries	$4,156,480
Coal	731,817
Ice	183,134
Total free States	**$5,071,431**

FREE AND SLAVE STATES.

Products of the forest	11,756,060
Products of agriculture	20,206,265
Vegetable food	25 656,494
Manufactures	35,154 644
Manufactured articles	2 397,031
Raw produce	1,355,805
Total free and slave States	**$96,826,290**

SLAVE STATES EXCLUSIVELY.

Cotton	$191,806,555
Tobacco	15,906,517
Rosin and turpentine	3,734,527
Rice	2,566,390
Tar and pitch	151,095
Brown sugar	103,244
Molasses	44,562
Hemp	8,951
Total slave States	**$214,322,880**

RECAPITULATION.

Free States exclusively	$5,071,431
Free and slave States	96,826,299
Slave States exclusively	214,322,880
Total	**$316,220,610**

If any one will analyze the articles embraced in the amount, $96,826,290, belonging alike to the North and the South, he cannot fail to come to the conclusion that at least one-third is justly the product of negro labor. The result, then, stands as follows ·

Exports of southern States	$246.598,313
Exports of northern "	69,622,297
Total	**$316,220,610**

Calling the population of the North, in round numbers, twenty millions, and the population of the South ten millions, we have the significant fact that while the exports of the North amount to only $3 45 per head, those of the South amount to $24 65!* It is not intended by this statement to deny that the North has vast industry, but white men, in a temperate or cold latitude, *consume* nearly all the products of their own labor, and hence it is,

* To this statement it may be objected that the North sends a vast quantity of produce and manufactured articles to the South, but it should be remembered that the South also sends a vast quantity of *her* produce North. Our consumption of cotton is about $55,000,000 ; of sugar; $25,000,000 ; besides naval stores, rice, tobacco, &c., which do not enter into our calculation of southern exports any more than the northern articles sent South enter into the exports of the North. Our calculation is based upon the *foreign* exports, as these only represent the *surplus* wealth of the country.

that in all ages, every nation which has acquired wealth and power, obtained them from tropical regions where the inferior races, in their normal relation to the superior race, produced them. It is thus self-evident that nearly all the wealth of our country is derived from negro servitude, for wealth is the surplus of production over consumption. The North has but little over—the South a great deal. It is the tropical regions which must be relied upon for this surplus wealth. When Spain held all her tropical possessions on this Continent, it is estimated that her net income from them was not less than $50,000,000 annually, and she was the mistress of the world.—When she lost them, her greatness and wealth declined, and she soon sunk to a third or fourth-rate power. Of late years she has been improving, and if she do not commit the folly of overthrowing the natural relation of the races, she will rapidly advance in power, wealth, and prosperity.

There is one other view of this question, which is very important, and is worthy the careful attention of every person who desires to be well informed upon the *causes* of the greatness, grandeur and prosperity of his country. It is frequently asserted, by shallow-minded people, who have never investigated this subject, that the North has supported the South, paid the expenses of the Government, &c. Now, all *imports* are based upon *exports*, and hence it is the *exports* which, in fact, furnish the revenue of a country and *not* the imports, for the latter are but the representative of the former, without which they could not exist. Taking the history of our government for forty years, this view of the case presents some most astounding results, which are condensed with much labor in the following table:

RETURNS FROM THE TREASURY DEPARTMENT AT WASHINGTON, SHOW-ING THE VALUE OF THE EXPORTS AND IMPORTS FOR FORTY YEARS, FROM 1821 TO 1861, WITH THE CUSTOMS PAID DURING THE SAME TIME TO THE UNITED STATES.

Gross Value of Exports, from 1821 to 1861	$5,556,401,273
" " Imports, " "	5,501,238,157
Customs Duties on Imports paid in the U. S. Treasury	1,191,874,443

TOTAL UNITED STATES EXPORTS FOR FORTY YEARS.

		Amount of Duty.
Cotton	$2,574,834,991	
Tobacco	424,118,067	
Rice	87,854,511	
Naval Stores	110,981,296	
	$3,193,850,965	$889,141,805
Food	1,006,951,835	216,682,773
Gold	458,588,615	95,849,955
Crude Articles, Manufactures, &c.	892,010,457	190,699,910
	$5,556,401,272	$1,191,874,443

EXPORTS FROM THE SOUTH EXCLUSIVELY, FOR FORTY YEARS.

		Amount of Duty, paid by the South.
Cotton	$2,574,834,091	
Tobacco	425,118,067	
Rice	87,854,511	
Naval Stores	110,951,296	$889,141,805
One third of Food	335,650,411	72,227,591
40 per cent. Gold *	183,588,615	88,189,982
	$3,718,026,991	$799,508,378
Amount of Duty from the North		392,365,065
Difference		$407,244,813

* Some people, without reflecting, may suppose that this estimate, giving the South one-third of the gold production for forty years, is too high; but they should recollect

It will thus be seen that southern products have contributed to the support of the government nearly $800,000,000, while northern products have contributed less than half that sum! Can there be any doubt, therefore, in the mind of any candid and sensible person, that this country owes its unparalleled prosperity to negro labor? We do not mean to say that this difference arises from any inferiority of northern or superiority of southern men, but solely from that *universal law of nature, that the cultivation of the tropics, carried on by the enforced labor of the inferior races, produces a large surplus over consumption, while white men in temperate latitudes consume nearly all they produce. Destroy this cultivation, and you destroy northern commerce, labor, mechanics, manufactures, &c., &c., and reduce white men to poverty and privation.*

The comparative value of free negro labor and "slave" negro labor is also forcibly illustrated in the *progress* of our own country, when compared with those places where the negro has been deprived of the guidance of the white man. It is often the habit of Abolition writers to compare the value of "free" and "slave" labor, in order to show the vast superiority of the former over the latter. But they are always very careful to have the comparison to occur between WHITE labor and negro labor. They never DARE to make a comparison between negro "FREE" labor and negro "SLAVE" labor. As white men are superior to negroes, their labor ought to be superior to theirs, and in all latitudes, where white labor is available, it is more valuable, because more intelligent. There is no sense, therefore, in comparing Ohio with Alabama, simply because there are no grounds for a comparison. The white man could not do the work of the negro in Alabama, nor could the negro do the work of the intelligent farmer in Ohio. The real question is, are the southern States in a better condition than the free negro countries? This is the correct test as to the success of free negroism. It is only necessary, in order to answer this question, to show the constant and steady increase of the great staple of cotton—a product that has done more for the comfort and happiness of the great toiling masses than any and all other productions of modern times:

Years.	Total Bales.	Export Value.
1800	35,000	$5,726,000
1824	509,158	21,947,401
1830	870,415	29,674,883
1835	1,254,328	64,961,302
1840	2,177,532	63,870,303
1845	2,394,503	51,739,643
1850	2,796,700	71,984,616
1851	2,355,257	112,315,317
1852	3,015,029	87,965,732
1853	3,262,832	109,456,404
1854	2,930,027	93,596,220
1855	2,847,339	88,143,844
1856	3,527,841	128,382,351
1857	2,939,519	131,575,859
1858	3,113,962	131,386,661
1859	3,851,481	161,434,923
1860	4,300,000	184,400,000

that the estimate is made for forty years, and we have had gold from California for only ten or twelve years. Previous to that time we depended entirely upon the mines of Georgia, North and South Carolina, Virginia, and Maryland for our gold. These mines have been very productive, the Dorn mine in South Carolina bringing to the U. S. Mint, at Charlotte, $220,000 to $225,000 annually.

What a grand and noble picture does not this present! Yet in 1817, the production of cotton in the West Indies and the United States was just about the same! and Wm. Lloyd Garrison, Geo. Thompson and Dr. Channing, at the time of the West India emancipation, predicted that free negro labor would soon drive all "slave" grown cotton out of the market! These architects of ruin, however, shut their eyes to the desolation they have achieved, and now, with the malignity of demons, desire to bring the calamities upon our own hitherto prosperous and happy country, which have marked the progress of the free negro delusion in other places.

The territory cursed by free negroism in the West Indies, however, is but a small portion of the space now blighted in the same manner. We have given no statistics of the condition of all that vast territory, comprising the fairest and most beautiful portion of our continent, extending from the Rio Grande almost to the Amazon. When it was under its Spanish conquerors, this territory, almost as large as the whole United States, was largely productive. Its capabilities, however, were never developed to anything like their full extent, yet such cultivation as was commenced has been almost wholly abandoned. The country may be truly described as a desert, with only here and there an oasis, where a rude kind of cultivation produces just enough to let the world know that it is not an entire waste. Brazil, on the south, is the first spot where commerce and trade exist to any great extent, and there the negro has not been freed. We are thus able to count up, with perfect ease, the only places where tropical production is now carried on on this Continent—Cuba, Porto Rico, our own Gulf States and Brazil! Just four comparatively small green spots amid the wild and uncultivated yet fertile and glorious tropical regions of the western hemisphere!

PART III.

THE EFFECT OF FREE NEGROISM UPON TRADE, COMMERCE, AGRICULTURE, AND WHITE LABOR.

No nation or people, from the days of imperial Babylon, has ever been great in wealth or power which did not possess the trade of the tropical regions of a continent. It is the wealth of the East Indies which has made England what she is. With the riches which poured into her coffers, from 1750, after she expelled the Dutch from India, she was enabled to crush Napoleon, and raise herself to that imperial power in the world which was formerly swayed by Rome. The rise and fall of imperial greatness in Asia and Europe has been determined by the possession of the trade of the East Indies, where the enforced labor of over two hundred millions of natives has formed an overflowing stream of wealth.

The Creator has intended our own tropical regions to be productive. They were not made "to waste their sweetness on the desert air." In His own way He had the negro brought here from Africa, where he had been a wild, untutored savage for centuries, just what he must and will be forever, when he is separated from the white man. This negro has been made available for just the work we need to be done. The white men of this continent need and MUST HAVE cotton, sugar, coffee, indigo, spices, &c., &c. Without these, civilization is put back five hundred years. True, we MIGHT again drag along as our ancestors did, the rich only being able to afford good clothing. The poor might manufacture their own by spinning, and carding, and weaving. Sugar, coffee, &c., might be again unknown luxuries. The farmer might have little or no market for his grains, but this would not satisfy us. These articles must be had, and they cannot be had without the enforced labor of the negro.

Already white men have been, and are to-day, seriously taxed for the laziness of this negro. Take the two items of sugar and coffee alone. If we estimate the decline in the production of sugar and coffee by the reduction that has taken place in Jamaica and other places, it is fair to calculate that, were all the negroes, now lolling in the sun, eating yams and laughing at white men, set to work, we should have at least THREE TIMES the amount of both articles now produced. Such a production would decrease the price at least ONE-HALF, thus furnishing the white men of this country with their groceries at 50 per cent. less than present prices.

Let us look at this subject a little more closely. The "grocery bill" of the people of the United States is annually $86,928,000. Our imports of coffee, sugar, tobacco and molasses, for 1850, amounted in value to $38,479,000, of which the negro "slaves" of Cuba and Brazil supplied $34,451,000. The balance of these four articles that we need, $48,449,000, is the product of our own "slave" States. The "grocery bill" of the people of the United States stands indebted as follows:—

To Negro "Slave" labor........................$82,900,000
To other sources.............................. 4,028,000

It is now proposed to wipe out this $82,000,000 —to "free" the negroes, as it is called, who are now industriously contributing their share to the civilization and happiness of mankind. If it be done, the result is apparent. All kinds of groceries will rise in price to such an extent that no one but the wealthy classes can afford to use them. THE "SLAVE" NEGRO IS THE POOR MAN'S FRIEND. THE "FREED" NEGRO IS HIS BITTER AND UNRELENTING ENEMY. If freed in the tropical regions, he ceases to produce anything, and all know that the less of an article produced, the higher the price, and of course the greater the tax upon the consumer. Every negro, therefore, lazily squatting in the West Indies, and, as the London Times says, "sniggering at Buckra," takes something from the pocket of every consumer of sugar, coffee and molasses. The cost of tropical productions is now fifty per cent above what it ought to be. Coffee ought to be had for about the tax now upon it, and sugar in proportion. We are paying nearly NINETY MILLIONS of dollars annually for our groceries—FORTY MILLIONS of it ought to be saved, and would be, if every negro was made to fulfill the Heaven-decreed ordinance of labor.

But the tax of free negroism upon the North is not fully seen in the increased price of coffee, sugar, tobacco, &c. Every negro freed in the tropics becomes at once a non-consumer of northern products. When at work on the plantation, he eats bacon and bread, and is furnished with plenty of good, coarse clothing, shoes, hats, &c. When freed, as we have shown, he eats yams and plantains mainly, and consumes little or nothing of northern productions. The farmer and mechanic, therefore, are not only taxed in one way, but in two ways—First, by an increase in the price of coffee, sugar,

&c.; and secondly, by a decrease in the DEMAND for their own productions.
It was not until the extension of "slavery" occurred in Alabama, Mississippi and Louisiana, that the western farmer began to get anything like
remunerative prices for his grain. And it is a singular fact that, despite
the howls of politicians, the column of black labor on the Gulf, and of white
labor above the 36th parallel of latitude, have kept right along *pari passu.*
The one is the handmaid of the other. Destroy "slavery" on the Gulf,
and you destroy the farmer in Ohio, Illinois, Indiana and Iowa. It would
be of little use to remove the blockade of the Mississippi if the negro is to
be freed. The demons of mischief have educated the northern mind to believe that there is an antagonism between what they call " free and slave
labor,"—that is, between white labor and negro labor. Now, should Beel-
zebub try to invent a falsehood exceeding all his former attempts in that
line, he could not do it so well as by adopting this one. The truth is, there
never was a more beautiful or perfect harmony in the world than that existing between white labor and negro labor, and when we say negro labor, we
mean what the Abolitionists and Republicans call "slave" labor, for there
is NO SUCH THING AS FREE NEGRO LABOR. The negro, as we have shown,
on a plantation, becomes a consumer of the agricultural productions of the
northern farmer, and the skilled labor of the northern mechanic. His labor
sets in motion cotton factories and machine shops. THE MUSCLES OF THE
NEGRO AND THE INTELLECT OF THE WHITE MAN THUS BECOME THE GREAT
AGENCIES OF MODERN CIVILIZATION. The exchange of the one for the other
constitutes OUR COMMERCE, gives employment to shipping, erects our banks,
lines our streets with marble palaces, and makes a rocky island like New
York, the seat of untold wealth. EVERY BRICK ON OUR STREETS IS CEMENTED
WITH THE LABOR OF THE NEGRO.

But people often say, is not the North great and powerful by herself? We
answer, no. What are all the productions of agriculture unless there is a
market for them? The matter can be illustrated thus: Suppose all the
negroes of Brazil, Cuba and the southern States from which we now derive
all our groceries, were set to raising grain, &c., for their own subsistence.
Of course, there would be no exchange of commodities and no commerce.
The world is constituted with different climates and productions for the pur-
poses of exchange and commerce. Each hemisphere has its temperate and
tropical regions, and those regions require different labor. To overthrow
that form of labor by which only the tropics can be cultivated is as criminal
as it would be to overthrow the system of labor necessary for the temperate
latitudes. The tropics can not be cultivated by "freed" negroes any more
than the temperate latitudes could be by putting white men in slavery.—
Looking to Europe as a market for our agricultural productions is a delusion. Each hemisphere of the world is mainly independent of the other.
For centuries they existed without the knowledge of each other, and if we
were to day utterly and forever separated from the Old World, it might be
quite as well for us. The anti-slavery imposture sprung from there, and
though we declared ourselves independent of the mother country, yet prac-
tically she has ruled us through her ideas, and is doing it to-day. The call
for our agricultural productions occurs perhaps in one year out of five, but
our real and permanent markets are the tropics of our own continent. If
every negro in Mexico, Central America, New Granada and the West Indies
were this day industriously at work, we judge each white laborer in the
North would have his wages increased one-half, while the cost of articles for
his family would be decreased in about the same ratio. The western farmer,

now getting only eight or ten cents per bushel for his corn, ought to, and would, then get twenty-five cents. Let each man, therefore, compute the expense of free negroism as it affects himself personally.—Persons earning $1 00 per day would, if the negro were doing *his* duty, get at least $1 50. If the grocery bill of a family is now $100 per year, it would then be £50, and so on in proportion. The laboring classes then, instead of living in close, ill-ventilated apartments, where the light of day is scarcely permitted to enter, might afford neat and agreeable cottages. The demoralization of huddling human beings together would be mainly obviated, and the education, intelligence and morality of the white population vastly increased. The greatest curse of free negroism is its effect upon WHITE MEN. It enslaves them, it binds burdens upon them, and if in contact with this free negro, ho becomes their legal equal, and among the debased and vicious leads to amalgamation. It makes Five Points in our cities, and blots and blasts our community like a sirocco. Philanthropists have dreamed of social reforms, of the elevation of the white laboring classes, and predicted a future wherein want should be unknown, and labor meet an adequate reward but they have been looking for it through social reforms, if not convulsions. The condition of tho laboring classes of Europe has been often bewailed, but our own are now fast reaching their position. Tho great want is remunerative labor. Where can it be had? is tho universal cry. Tho farmer wants better prices for his grain, the mechanic for his labor. Why do they not get them? The answer is summed up in two words, FREE NEGROISM! This destroys commerce. This decreases the demand for white labor. This closes up the market of the farmer, and enables some Shylock, who holds a mortgage upon his farm, to turn his wife and children out of doors.

And yet it is gravely supposed by the President of the United States to be a very desirable object to set some four millions more of negroes, what is called, free. Ho even proposes to have white men take out their pocket books and pay for the luxury of taxing themselves for the purchase of these negroes. The scheme ho has proposed is one of the most astounding that could ever havo issued from a sane mind. It is proposed to pay $300 per head for these negroes. Taking the whole 4,000,000, this would amount to twelve hundred millions of dollars, which would be a tax of $40 upon *every white man, woman and child* in the whole United States! When this is done, what have we got for our money? Well, the facts we have collected in the foregoing pages enable us to answer this question in such a manner that no "white man, though a fool, need err therein."

1st. We shall have a population which will labor at no productive employment, but insist on living on the labor of the whites. This is one tax.

2nd. Vice, crime and pauperism are six or eight times as prevalent among thom as among whites. The second tax.

3d. By setting them free from all control, they have ceased producing the articles wo need, and we are forced to pay a higher price for them. This is the third tax.

4th. The abstraction of these productions from the world decreases just so much the wealth of the world, and of course lessens business. Here is a fourth tax.

5th. Tho negroes thus set "free" in all tho tropical regions cease to be consumers of the products of our farmers and mechanics, and hence the demand for northern productions of all kinds is lessened. Here is a fifth tax.

Now, a person, when he purchases anything, expects to get some value for his money, some profit on the investment. But here we have paid our money, for what? For value received? No, but for the privilege of taxing ourselves in at least *five distinct ways and forms*. And it is a tax that falls upon every man, woman and child in the land. It blights every fireside. It stands like a spectre at every threshold. It can no more be avoided than death. It comes in every thing we eat, in every thing wo drink, and in every thing we wear.

The farmer pays for the idleness of the negro in every pound of sugar or coffee ho buys, and in every bushel of wheat or corn he sells. The mechanic pays for it in low prices for his labor and high prices for his groceries.

Shall we, therefore, go on in this mad career of folly and crime? Shall we shut our eyes, to facts, and in sheer party madness rush on to national suicide? All around us are scattered the ruins of free negroism. Torn and distracted Mexico. Desolate and wild Central America. Silent and deserted Now Granada. Ruined and savage Hayti. Dilapidated and broken-down Jamaica, all testify in thunder tones to beware of the breakers of free negroism. On the contrary, Brazil, Cuba, Porto Rico and the southern States are the marts of commerce and trade. Wherever the negro occupies his true and normal relation to the white man, all is happiness and prosperity. Where he does not, all is social chaos and blight. The relation that the negro race shall occupy to the white thus becomes the most important question ever presented to the WHITE MEN OF AMERICA. On its decision hangs the fate of republican institutions as well as the national happiness and well-being of the white masses. The GREAT DELUSION of the nineteenth century is approaching its climax, and if it shall bo reached without overturning the social order, which, for two hundred years, has worked out such boundless blessings and such untold prosperity to all classes of our people, we may confidently anticipate a renewal and even an advance of that prosperity. But, if the reverse take place, no pen can describo the chaos, confusion, poverty and degradation which, as a legacy, we shall transmit to our children. If the foregoing pages shall contribute, in any degree whatover, towards preventing these calamities falling upon the WHITE MEN OF AMERICA, tho object of the writer of this pamphlet will have been accomplished.

ANTI-ABOLITION WORKS.

SOUTHERN WEALTH

AND

NORTHERN PROFITS;

As Exhibited by Statistical Facts and Official Figures.

By THOMAS PRENTICE KETTEL, late Editor of the "Democratic Review."
Complete in one Octavo Volume, bound in Cloth,
75 cents, or in Paper Covers, 50 cents.

DRED SCOTT DECISION.

Opinion of Chief-Justice TANEY, with an Introduction by Dr. J. H. VAN EVRIE.
Also, an Appendix, containing an Essay on the Natural History of
the Prognathous Race of Mankind, by Dr. S. A. CART-
WRIGHT, of New Orleans. Pamphlet, 48
pages, octavo. Price, 25 cents.

NEGRO SLAVERY NOT UNJUST.

Speech of CHARLES O'CONOR, Esq., at the great Union Meeting in
New York city, in 1859. Pamphlet, octavo,
16 pages. Price six cents.

☞ *Any of the above works will be sent by mail, postage
free, on receipt of price.*

VAN EVRIE, HORTON & CO., Publishers,
No. 162 NASSAU STREET, New York.

ANTI-ABOLITION TRACTS.

For twenty-five or thirty years, the Abolitionists have deluged the country with innumerable books, pamphlets, and tracts inculcating their false and pernicious doctrines. Little or nothing has ever been done in the same way towards counteracting their influence. Thousands now feel that such publications are indispensably necessary. In order to supply what it is believed is a wide-felt want, the undersigned have determined to issue a series of "Anti-Abolition Tracts," embracing a concise discussion of current political issues, in such a cheap and popular form, and at such a merely nominal price for large quantities, as ought to secure for them a very extensive circulation. Two numbers of these Tracts have already been issued. No. 1 gives a critical analysis of the real causes of our present deplorable difficulties, and shows how, and how only, the Union can be restored. No. 2 is a brief history of the Results of Emancipation, showing its wretched and miserable future, ant that Negro Freedom is simply a tax upon White Labor. The facts in relation to the real condition of the Freed Negroes in Hayti, Jamaica, etc., have been carefully suppressed by the Abolition papers, but they ought to be laid before the public at once, so that the evils which now afflict Mexico, Hayti, and all countries where the Negro-equalizing doctrines have been tried, may be averted from our country forever.

No. 1.—ABOLITION AND SECESSION: or Cause and Effect, together with the Remedy for our Sectional Troubles. By a Unionist.

No. 2.—FREE NEGROISM: or Results of Emancipation in the North and the West India Islands; with Statistics of the Decay of Commerce, Idleness of the Negro, his Return to Savagism, and the Effect of Emancipation upon the Farming, Mechanical, and Laboring Classes.

TERMS:

Single copies...$0 06
Twenty copies.. 1 00
One hundred copies... 4 00

All orders under 100, at the rates named, will be sent by mail, post paid. All orders for 100 or over will be sent by express, or as may be directed by the party ordering, at his own expense. Very liberal discount made where a thousand copies or over are ordered at one time. Address

VAN EVRIE, HORTON & CO., *Publishers,*

No. 162 Nassau St., N. Y.

The Publishers earnestly request all in whose hands these TRACTS may fall, if they think they will do good, to aid in circulating them. We have taken the liberty to send specimen copies to many persons, for their perusal, hoping that they will assist in this important work. We would also esteem it a favor if they will have the goodness to state the terms on which they are published, for the convenience of others who may feel inclined to order copies for sale or gratuitous distribution.

www.ingramcontent.com/pod-product-compliance
Lightning Source LLC
Chambersburg PA
CBHW021604270326
41931CB00009B/1366